The Constitution of the Republic of Albania

Prepared and Introduced by
Yusuf Hashani

CS Publishing, 2018

Copyright © 2018 by Yusuf Hashani

First Published in April, 2018
by CSI Publishing
All rights reserved. Except for the constitution,
no part of this publication may be reproduced, stored
in any retrieval system, or transmitted, in any form or by
any means, electronic, mechanical, photocopying, recording or otherwise
without the prior permission of the editor.
Prepared by Yusuf Hashani
Typeset by the editor

ISBN-10:171739938X
Available
Constitution – Albania
Cover artwork: Flag of Albania

Table of Contents

Introduction
Map
Common Political Acronyms in Albania
Albanian Alphabet and Transliteration Chart
Constitution

Introduction

The present-day Republic of Albania is located in Southeastern Europe. The country spans 28,748 square kilometers (11,100 square miles) and has a total population of 3 million as of 2016. The capital of the country is Tirana.[1]

The Constitution of Albania was adopted by the Parliament of the country on November 28th, 1998. The document succeeded the 1976 Constitution, originally adopted at the formation of the People's Socialist Republic of Albania on the 28th of December that same year. The document was heavily amended in 1991.

The Constitution defines the country as a unitary parliamentary constitutional republic. The document itself is divided into a number of parts which sanction a parliamentary democracy, people's sovereignty and fundamental rights of the citizens as a whole.

Due to political instability through the years, Albania has had a number of constitutions. After its independence in 1912, the nation was initially constituted as a monarchy in 1913, briefly a republic in the 1920s, then it returned to a democratic monarchy in 1928. It later became a socialist republic until the restoration of capitalism and democracy in the 1990s.

---

[1] For more on Albania, see *Albania in a Nutshell: A Brief History and Chronology of Events* by Robert Elsie.

Map: Albania and the Region

Common Political Acronyms in Albania

AD - Aleanca Demokratike (Democratic Alliance)

APC - Albanian Communist Party

DBSH - E Djathta e Bashkuar Shqiptare (United Albanian Right)

LSI - Lëvizja Socialiste për Integrim (Socialist Movement for Intregration)

PAA - Partia Agrare Ambientaliste (Agrarian Environmentalist Party)

PAD - Partia Aleanca Demokratike (Democratic Alliance Party)

PALSH - Partia Alternativa Liberale Shqiptare (Albanian Liberal Alternative Party)

PASH - Partia Agrare Shqiptare (Albanian Agrarian Party)

PBD - Partia Bashkimi Demokratik (Democratic Union Party)

PBDNJ - Partia Bashkimi për të Drejtat e Njeriut (Union for Human Rights Party)

PBK - Partia Balli Kombëtar (National Front Party)

PBKD - Partia Balli Kombetar Demokrat (Democratic National Front Party)

PBKSH - Partia Bashkësia Kombëtare Shqiptare (Albanian National Unity Party)

PBKSH - Partia e Bashkuar Komuniste Shqiptare (United Albanian Communist Party)

PBL - Partia Bashkimi Liberal (Liberal Union Party)

PBRSH - Partia Bashkimi Republikan Shqiptar (Albanian Republican Union Party)

PBSD - Partia Bashkimi Socialdemokrat (Social Democratic Union Party)

PBSH - Partia e Biznesit Shqiptar (Albanian Business Party)

PD - Partia Demokratike (Democratic Party)

PDD - Partia e Djathtë Demokrate (Democratic Right Party)

PDI - Partia për Drejtësi dhe Integrim (Party for Justice and Integration)

PDK - Partia Demokristiane e Shqipërisë (Christian Democratic Party of Albania)

PDR - Partia Demokratike e Re (New Democratic Party)

PDS - Partia Demokracia Sociale e Shqipërisë (Social Democracy Party of Albania)

PDSH - Partia Demokratike e Shqipërisë (Democratic Party of Albania)

PESH - Partia e Emigracionit Shqiptar (Albanian Emigration Party)

PFA - Partia Forca Albania (Forca Albania Party)

PKONS - Partia Konservatore (Conservative Party)

PKSH - Partia Komuniste Shqiptare (Albanian Communist Party)

PLD - Partia Lëvizja për Demokraci (Movement for Democracy Party)

PLFSH - Partia Lidhja Fshatare Shqiptare (Albanian Rural League Party)

PLL - Partia Lëvizja e Legalitetit (Movement for Legality Party)

PLPSH - Partia Lëvizja Punëtore Shqiptare (Albanian Labor Movement Party)

PMP - Partia e Mirëqenies Popullore (People's Welfare Party)

PPD - Partia Progresi Demokratik (Democratic Progress Party)

PPK - Partia e Pajtimit Kombëtar Shqiptar (Albanian National Reconciliation Party)

PPSH - Partia e Punës e Shqipërisë (Party of Labor of Albania)

PRDSH - Partia Reformatore Demokratike Shqiptare (Albanian Democratic Reform Party)

PRSH - Partia Republikane Shqiptare (Albanian Republican Party)

PSDSH - Partia Socialdemokrate e Shqipërisë (Social Democratic Party of Albania)

PSHA - Partia Shqiptare Ambientaliste (Albanian Environmentalist Party)

PSI - Partia Socialiste për Integrim (Socialist Party for Integration)

PSKSH - Partia Socialkristiane Shqiptare (Albanian Social Christian Party)

PSSH - Partia Socialiste e Shqiperisë (Socialist Party of Albania)

PUKSH - Partia e Unitetit Kombëtar Shqiptar (Albanian National Unity Party)

Albanian Alphabet and Transliteration Chart

Letters		Read as	Pronounce	Albanian Examples	English equivalent
A	a	a	a	af__ë__r	f__a__r
B	b	bë	b	buk__ë__	__b__at
C	c	cë	ts	ceremoni	i__ts__y
Ç	ç	ë	tʃ	çelës	__ch__at
D	d	dë	d	dasëm	__d__oor
Dh	dh	dhë	ð	dhelpër	__th__ere
E	e	e	e	emër	__e__nter
Ë	ë	ë	ə	ëmbël	__a__round
F	f	fë	f	fletë	__f__ly
G	g	gë	g	gurë	__g__um
Gj	gj	gjë	ɟ	gjeneral	__j__oin
H	h	hë	h	hap	__h__at
I	i	i	i	jep	s__ea__
J	j	jë	j	javë	__y__awn
K	k	kë	k	këmishë	__k__ite
L	l	lë	l	lopë	__l__eave
Ll	ll	llë	ɫ or l	llampë	mi__ll__
M	m	më	m	mal	__m__an
N	n	në	n	nënë	__n__o
Nj	nj	një	ɲ	njeri	o__ni__on
O	o	o	o	orë	__o__pen
P	p	pë	p	parti	__p__en
Q	q	që	q	qumësht	ma__t__ure
R	r	rë	ɾ	raport	__r__ed
Rr	rr	rrë	r (rolled)	rrjesht	bo__rr__ow
S	s	së	s	stacion	__s__top
Sh	sh	shë	ʃ	shtëpi	__sh__op
T	t	të	t	televizion	__t__ree
Th	th	thë	θ	thupër	__th__in
U	u	u	u	urë	f__oo__d
V	v	vë	v	vezë	__v__est
X	x	xë	dz	xixë	ad__z__e
Xh	xh	xhë	dʒ	xhaxha	__J__upiter
Y	y	y	y	yll	n__ew__
Z	z	z	z	zemër	__z__ebra
Zh	zh	zhë	ʒ	zhurmë	plea__s__ure

The Constitution of the Republic of Albania

We, the people of Albania, proud and aware of our history, with responsibility for the future, and with faith in God and/or other universal values,

with determination to build a social and democratic state based on the rule of law, and to guarantee the fundamental human rights and freedoms,

with a spirit of religious coexistence and tolerance,

with a pledge to protect human dignity and personhood, as well as for the prosperity of the whole nation, for peace, well-being, culture and social solidarity,

with the centuries-old aspiration of the Albanian people for national identity and unity,

with a deep conviction that justice, peace, harmony and cooperation between nations are among the highest values of humanity,

We establish this Constitution:

PART ONE--BASIC PRINCIPLES

Article 1

1. Albania is a parliamentary republic.
2. The Republic of Albania is a unitary and indivisible state.
3. Governance is based on a system of elections that are free, equal, general and periodic.

Article 2

1. Sovereignty in the Republic of Albania belongs to the people.
2. The people exercise sovereignty through their representatives or directly.
3. For the maintenance of peace and national interests, the Republic of Albania may take part in a system of collective security, on the basis of a law approved by a majority of all the members of the Assembly.

Article 3

The independence of the state and the integrity of its territory, the dignity of the person, his rights and freedoms, social justice, the constitutional order, pluralism, national identity and inheritance, religious coexistence, and coexistence with, and understanding of Albanians for, minorities are the bases of this state, which has the duty of respecting and protecting them.

Article 4

1. The law constitutes the basis and the boundaries of the activity of the state.
2. The Constitution is the highest law in the Republic of Albania.
3. The provisions of the Constitution are directly applicable, except when the Constitution provides otherwise.

Article 5

The Republic of Albania applies international law that is binding upon it.

Article 6

The organization and operation of the organs contemplated by this Constitution are regulated by their respective laws, except when this Constitution provides otherwise.

Article 7

The system of government in the Republic of Albania is based on the separation and balancing of legislative, executive and judicial powers.

Article 8

1. The Republic of Albania protects the national rights of the Albanian people who live outside its borders.
2. The Republic of Albania protects the rights of its citizens with a temporary or permanent residence outside its borders.
3. The Republic of Albania assures assistance for Albanians who live and work abroad in order to preserve and develop their ties with the national cultural inheritance.

Article 9

1. Political parties are created freely. Their organization shall conform with democratic principles.
2. Political parties and other organizations, the programs and activity of which are based on totalitarian methods, which incite and support racial, religious, regional or ethnic hatred, which use violence to take power or influence state policy, as well as those with a secret character, are prohibited pursuant to the law.
3. The sources of financing of parties as well as their expenses are always made public.

Article 10

1. In the Republic of Albania there is no official religion.
2. The state is neutral on questions of belief and conscience and guarantees the freedom of their expression in public life.
3. The state recognizes the equality of religious communities.
4. The state and the religious communities mutually respect the independence of one another and work together for the good of each and all.
5. Relations between the state and religious communities are regulated on the basis of agreements entered into between their representatives and the Council of Ministers. These agreements are ratified by the Assembly.
6. Religious communities are juridical persons. They have independence in the administration of their properties according to their principles, rules and canons, to the extent that interests of third parties are not infringed.

Article 11

1. The economic system of the Republic of Albania is based on private and public property, as well as on a market economy and on freedom of economic activity.
2. Private and public property are equally protected by law.
3. Limitations on the freedom of economic activity may be established only by law and for important public reasons.

Article 12

1. The armed forces guarantee the independence of the country, and protect its territorial integrity and constitutional order.
2. The armed forces maintain neutrality in political questions and are subject to civilian control.
3. No foreign military force may be situated in, or pass through, the Albanian territory, and no Albanian military force may be sent abroad, except by a law approved by a majority of all members of the Assembly.

Article 13

Local government in the Republic of Albania is founded upon the basis of the principle of decentralization of power and is exercised according to the principle of local autonomy.

Article 14

1. The official language in the Republic of Albania is Albanian.
2. The national flag is red with a two-headed black eagle in the center.
3. The seal of the Republic of Albania is a red shield with a black, two-headed eagle in the center. At the top of the shield, in gold, is the helmet of Skanderbeg.
4. The national anthem is "United Around Our Flag."
5. The National Holiday of the Republic of Albania is Flag Day, November 28.
6. The capital city of the Republic of Albania is Tirana.
7. The form and dimensions of the national symbols, the content of the text of the national anthem, and their use shall be regulated by law.

PART TWO--FUNDAMENTAL HUMAN RIGHTS AND FREEDOMS

CHAPTER I--GENERAL PRINCIPLES

Article 15

1. The fundamental human rights and freedoms are indivisible, inalienable, and inviolable and stand at the base of the entire juridical order.
2. The organs of public power, in fulfillment of their duties, shall respect the fundamental rights and freedoms, as well as contribute to their realization.

Article 16

1. The fundamental rights and freedoms and the duties contemplated in this Constitution for Albanian citizens are also valid for foreigners and stateless persons in the territory of the Republic of Albania, except for cases when the Constitution specifically attaches the exercise of particular rights and freedoms with Albanian citizenship.
2. The fundamental rights and freedoms and the duties contemplated in this Constitution are valid also for juridical persons so long as they comport with the general purposes of these persons and with the core of these rights, freedoms and duties.

Article 17

1. Limitations of the rights and freedoms provided for in this Constitution may be established only by law, in the public interest or for the protection of the rights of others. A limitation shall be in proportion to the situation that has dictated it.
2. These limitations may not infringe the essence of the rights and freedoms and in no case may exceed the limitations provided for in the European Convention on Human Rights.

Article 18

1. All are equal before the law.
2. No one may be unjustly discriminated against for reasons such as gender, race, religion, ethnicity, language, political, religious or philosophical beliefs, economic condition, education, social status, or parentage.
3. No one may be discriminated against for the reasons mentioned in paragraph 2 without a reasonable and objective justification.

Article 19

1. Everyone born of at least one parent with Albanian citizenship gains Albanian citizenship automatically. Albanian citizenship is gained also for other reasons provided by law.
2. An Albanian citizen cannot lose his citizenship, except when he relinquishes it.

Article 20

1. Persons who belong to national minorities exercise the human rights and freedoms in full equality before the law.
2. They have the right freely to express, without prohibition or compulsion, their ethnic, cultural, religious and linguistic belonging. They have the right to preserve and develop them, to study and to be taught in their mother tongue, and to unite in organizations and associations for the protection of their interests and identity.

CHAPTER II--PERSONAL RIGHTS AND FREEDOMS

Article 21

The life of the person is protected by law.

Article 22

1. Freedom of expression is guaranteed.
2. Freedom of the press, radio and television is guaranteed.
3. Prior censorship of means of communication is prohibited.
4. The law may require authorization to be granted for the operation of radio or television stations.

Article 23

1. The right to information is guaranteed.
2. Everyone has the right, in compliance with law, to obtain information about the activity of state organs, and of persons who exercise state functions.
3. Everyone is given the possibility to attend meetings of elected collective organs.

Article 24

1. Freedom of conscience and of religion is guaranteed.
2. Everyone is free to choose or to change his religion or beliefs, as well as to express them individually or collectively, in public or private life, through cult, education, practices or the performance of rituals.
3. No one may be compelled or prohibited to take part in a religious community or its practices or to make his beliefs or faith public.

Article 25

No one may be subjected to torture, cruel, inhuman or degrading punishment or treatment.

Article 26

No one may be required to perform forced labor, except in cases of the execution of a judicial decision, the performance of military service, or for a service that results from a state of war, a state of emergency or a natural disaster that threatens human life or health.

Article 27

1. No one's liberty may be taken away except in the cases and according to the procedures provided by law.
2. The liberty of a person may not be limited, except in the following cases:
   a. when he is punished with imprisonment by a competent court;
   b. for failure to comply with the lawful orders of the court or with an obligation set by law;
   c. when there is a reasonable suspicion that he has committed a criminal offense or to prevent the commission by him of a criminal offense or his escape after its commission;
   ç. for the supervision of a minor for purposes of education or for escorting him to a competent organ;
   d. when a person is the carrier of a contagious disease, mentally incompetent and dangerous to society;
   dh. for illegal entry at state borders or in cases of deportation or extradition.
3. No one may be deprived of liberty just because he is not in a state to fulfill a contractual obligation.

Article 28

1. Everyone whose liberty has been taken away has the right to be notified immediately, in a language that he understands, of the reasons for this measure, as well as the accusation made against him. The person whose liberty has been taken away shall be informed that he has no obligation to make a declaration and has the right to communicate immediately with his lawyer, and he shall also be given the possibility to exercise his rights.
2. The person whose liberty has been taken away, according to article 27, paragraph 2, subparagraph c, must be brought within 48 hours before a judge, who shall decide upon his pre-sentence detention or release not later than 48 hours from the moment he receives the documents for review.
3. A person in pre-sentence detention has the right to appeal the judge's decision. He has the right to be tried within a reasonable period of time or to be released on bail pursuant to law.
4. In all other cases, the person whose liberty is taken away extra judicially may address a judge at any time, who shall decide within 48 hours regarding the legality of this action.
5. Every person whose liberty was taken away pursuant to article 27 has the right to humane treatment and respect for his dignity.

Article 29

1. No one may be accused or declared guilty of a criminal offense that was not provided for by law at the time of its commission, with the exception of offenses, which at the time of their commission constituted war crimes or crimes against humanity according to international law.
2. No punishment may be given that is more severe than that which was contemplated by law at the time of commission of the criminal offense.
3. A favorable criminal law has retroactive effect.

Article 30

Everyone is deemed innocent so long as his guilt is not proven by final judicial decision.

Article 31

In a criminal proceeding, everyone has the right:
a. to be notified immediately and in detail of the charges against him, of his rights, and to have the possibility created to notify his family or relatives;
b. to have sufficient time and facilities to prepare his defense;
c. to have the assistance of a translator without charge, when he does not speak or understand the Albanian language;
ç. to be defended by himself or with the assistance of a legal defender chosen by him; to communicate freely and privately with him, as well as to be provided free defense when he does not have sufficient means;
d. to question witnesses who are present and to seek the appearance of witnesses, experts and other persons who can clarify the facts.

Article 32

1. No one may be compelled to testify against himself or his family or to confess his guilt.
2. No one may be declared guilty on the basis of data collected in an unlawful manner.

Article 33

1. Everyone has the right to be heard before being sentenced.
2. A person who is evading justice may not take advantage of this right.

Article 34

No one may be sentenced more than once for the same criminal offense or be tried again, except for cases when the re-adjudication of the case is ordered by a higher court, in the manner specified by law.

Article 35

1. No one may be compelled, except when the law requires it, to make public data related to his person.
2. The collection, use and making public of data about a person is done with his consent, except for the cases provided by law.
3. Everyone has the right to become acquainted with data collected about him, except for the cases provided by law.
4. Everyone has the right to request the correction or deletion of untrue or incomplete data or data collected in violation of law.

Article 36

The freedom and secrecy of correspondence or any other means of communication are guaranteed.

Article 37

1. The inviolability of the residence is guaranteed.
2. Searches of a residence, as well as premises that are equivalent to it, may be done only in the cases and manner provided by law.
3. No one may be subjected to a personal search outside a criminal proceeding, with the exception of cases of entry into, or exit from, the territory of the state, or to avoid a danger that threatens public security.

Article 38

1. Everyone has the right to choose his place of residence and to move freely to any part of the territory of the state.
2. No one may be hindered from leaving the state freely.

Article 39

1. No Albanian citizen may be expelled from the territory of the state.
2. Extradition may be permitted only when it is expressly provided in international agreements, to which the Republic of Albania is a party, and only by judicial decision.
3. The collective expulsion of foreigners is prohibited. The expulsion of foreign individuals is permitted under the conditions specified by law.

Article 40

Foreigners have the right of asylum in the Republic of Albania according to law.

Article 41

1. The right of private property is guaranteed.
2. Property may be acquired by gift, inheritance, purchase, or any other classical means provided by the Civil Code.
3. The law may provide for expropriations or limitations in the exercise of a property right only in the public interest.
4. Expropriations or limitations of a property right that amount to expropriation are permitted only against fair compensation.
5. In the case of disagreements related to the amount of compensation, a complaint may be filed in court.

Article 42

1. The liberty, property, and rights recognized in the Constitution and by law may not be infringed without due process.
2. Everyone, to protect his constitutional and legal rights, freedoms, and interests, or in the case of charges against him, has the right to a fair and public trial, within a reasonable time, by an independent and impartial court specified by law.

Article 43

Everyone has the right to appeal a judicial decision to a higher court, except when the Constitution provides otherwise.

Article 44

Everyone has the right to be rehabilitated and/or indemnified in compliance with law if he has been damaged because of an unlawful act, action or failure to act of the state organs.

CHAPTER III--POLITICAL RIGHTS AND FREEDOMS

Article 45

1. Every citizen who has reached the age of 18, even on the date of the elections, has the right to vote and to be elected.

2. Citizens who have been declared mentally incompetent by a final court decision do not have the right to vote.
3. Convicts who are serving a prison sentence have only the right to vote.
4. The vote is personal, equal, free and secret.

Article 46

1. Everyone has the right to organize collectively for any lawful purpose.
2. The registration of organizations or associations in court is done according to the procedure provided by law.
3. Organizations or associations that pursue unconstitutional purposes are prohibited pursuant to law.

Article 47

1. The freedom to have peaceful meetings, without arms, and to participate in them is guaranteed.
2. Peaceful meetings in squares and places of public passage are held in accordance with procedures provided by law.

Article 48

Everyone, by himself or together with others, may address requests, complaints or comments to the public organs, which are obliged to answer within the time periods and under the conditions set by law.

CHAPTER IV--ECONOMIC, SOCIAL AND CULTURAL RIGHTS AND FREEDOMS

Article 49

1. Everyone has the right to earn the means of living by lawful work that he has chosen or accepted himself. He is free to choose his profession, place of work, and his own system of professional qualification.
2. Employees have the right to social protection of labor.

Article 50

Employees have the right to unite freely in labor organizations for the defense of their work-related interests.

Article 51

1. The right of an employee to strike in connection with labor relations is guaranteed.
2. Limitations on particular categories of employees may be established by law to ensure essential social services.

Article 52

1. Everyone has the right to social security in old age or when he is unable to work, according to a system set by law.
2. Everyone who is without work involuntarily, and has no other means of support, has the right to assistance under the conditions provided by law.

Article 53

1. Everyone has the right to marry and have a family.
2. Marriage and family enjoy special protection of the state.
3. Marriage and divorce are regulated by law.

Article 54

1. Children, the young, pregnant women and new mothers have the right to special protection by the state.
2. Children born out of wedlock have rights equal to those born within marriage.
3. Every child has the right to be protected from violence, ill treatment, exploitation and from performing any work, especially under the minimum age for child labor, which could damage his health and morals or endanger his life or normal development.

Article 55

1. Citizens enjoy in an equal manner the right to health care from the state.
2. Everyone has the right to health insurance in accordance with the procedure provided by law.

Article 56

Everyone has the right to be informed about the status of the environment and its protection.

Article 57

1. Everyone has the right to education.
2. Mandatory education is set by law.
3. General high school public education is open to all.
4. Professional high school education and higher education can be conditioned only on merit.
5. Mandatory education and general high school education in public schools are free of charge.
6. Pupils and students may also be educated in non-public schools at all levels, which are created and operate on the basis of law.
7. The autonomy of institutions of higher education and academic freedom are guaranteed by law.

Article 58

1. The freedom of artistic creation and scientific research, their application, and the benefits from their achievements are guaranteed for all.
2. Copyright is protected by law.

CHAPTER V--SOCIAL OBJECTIVES

Article 59

1. The state, within its constitutional powers and the means at its disposal, and to supplement private initiative and responsibility, aims at:
   a. employment under suitable conditions for all persons who are able to work;
   b. fulfillment of the housing needs of its citizens;
   c. the highest possible standard of physical and mental health;
   ç. education and qualification of children and the young, as well as unemployed persons, according to their abilities;
   d. a healthy and ecologically adequate environment for the present and future generations;
   dh. the rational exploitation of forests, waters, pastures and other natural resources on the basis of the principle of sustainable development;
   e. care and help for the aged, orphans and persons with disabilities;
   ë. the development of sport and recreational activities;
   f. health rehabilitation, specialized education and integration of disabled people into society, and continual improvement of their living conditions;
   g. the protection of national cultural heritage and particular care for the Albanian language.
2. Fulfillment of social objectives cannot be claimed directly in court. The law defines under what conditions and to what extent the realization of these objectives can be claimed.

CHAPTER VI--PEOPLE'S ADVOCATE

Article 60

1. The People's Advocate defends the rights, freedoms and legitimate interests of individuals from unlawful or improper action or failure to act of the organs of public administration.
2. The People's Advocate is independent in the exercise of his duties.
3. The People's Advocate has a separate budget, which he administers himself. He proposes the budget pursuant to law.

Article 61

1. The People's Advocate is elected by three-fifths of all members of the Assembly for a five-year period, with the right of reelection.
2. Any Albanian citizen with higher education, and with recognized activity and knowledge in the field of human rights and law, may be the People's Advocate.
3. The People's Advocate enjoys the immunity of a judge of the High Court.
4. The People's Advocate may not take part in any political party, carry on any other political, state or professional activity, or take part in the management organs of social, economic and commercial organizations.

Article 62

1. The People's Advocate may be discharged only on the reasoned request of not less than one-third of the deputies.
2. In this case, the Assembly makes a decision with three-fifths of all its members.

Article 63

1. The People's Advocate presents an annual report before the Assembly.
2. The People's Advocate reports before the Assembly when so requested, and he may request the Assembly to hear him on matters he considers important.
3. The People's Advocate has the right to make recommendations and to propose measures when he finds violations of human rights and freedoms by the public administration.
4. Public organs and officials are obligated to provide the People's Advocate with all the documents and information requested by him.

PART THREE--THE ASSEMBLY

CHAPTER I--ELECTION AND TERM

Article 64

1. The Assembly consists of 140 deputies. One hundred deputies are elected directly in single member electoral zones with an approximately equal number of voters. Forty deputies are elected from multi-name lists of parties or party coalitions according to their ranking.
2. The total number of deputies of a party or a party coalition shall be, to the closest possible extent, proportional to the valid votes won by them on the national scale in the first round of elections.
3. Parties that receive less than 2.5 per cent, and party coalitions that receive less than 4 per cent, of the valid votes on the national scale in the first round of elections do not benefit from the respective multi-name list.

Article 65

1. The Assembly is elected for four years.
2. Elections for the Assembly are held 60 to 30 days before the end of the mandate and not later than 45 days after its dissolution.
3. The mandate of the Assembly continues until the first meeting of the new Assembly. In this interval, the Assembly may not issue laws or take decisions, except when extraordinary measures have been established.

Article 66

The mandate of the Assembly is extended only in case of war and for so long as it continues. When the Assembly has been dissolved, it re-convenes.

Article 67

1. The newly elected Assembly is called to its first meeting by the President of the Republic no later than 20 days from the conclusion of the elections.
2. If the President of the Republic does not exercise this power, the Assembly shall convene within 10 days from the end of the term provided in paragraph 1 of this article.

CHAPTER II--THE D EPUTIES

Article 68

1. Candidates for deputy may be presented only by political parties, coalitions of parties, and by voters.
2. The rules for the designation of candidates for deputy, for the organization and conduct of elections, and for the definition of electoral zones and the conditions of validity for elections are regulated by the electoral law.

Article 69

1. Without resigning from duty, the following may not run as candidates or be elected deputies:
    a. judges and prosecutors;
    b. military servicemen on active duty;
    c. staff of the police and of the national security;
    ç. diplomatic representatives;
    d. mayors of municipalities and communes as well as prefects in the places where they carry out their duties;
    dh. chairmen and members of the electoral commissions;
    e. the President of the Republic and the high officials of the state administration contemplated by law.
2. A mandate won in violation of paragraph 1 of this article is invalid.

Article 70

1. Deputies represent the people and are not bound by any obligatory mandate.
2. Deputies may not simultaneously exercise any other public duty with the exception of that of a member of the Council of Ministers. Other cases of incompatibility are specified by law.
3. Deputies may not carry out any profit- making activity that stems from the property of the state or of local government, and may not acquire the property of either of the latter.
4. For every violation of paragraph 3 of this article, on the motion of the Speaker of the Assembly or of one-tenth of its members, the Assembly decides on sending the case to the Constitutional Court, which decides on the incompatibility.

Article 71

1. The mandate of the deputy begins on the day when he is declared elected by the respective electoral commission.
2. The mandate of the deputy ends or is invalid, as the case may be: a. when he does not take the oath;

b. when he relinquishes the mandate;
c. when one of the conditions of ineligibility or incompatibility contemplated in articles 69 and 70, paragraphs 2 and 3, is ascertained;
ç. when the mandate of the Assembly ends;
d. when he is absent from the Assembly for more than six consecutive months without reason;
dh. when he is convicted by final court decision for the commission of a crime.

Article 72

Before beginning the mandate, the deputies take the oath in the Assembly.

Article 73

1. A deputy does not bear responsibility for opinions expressed in the Assembly and votes cast. This provision is not applicable in the case of defamation.
2. A deputy may not be criminally prosecuted without the authorization of the Assembly. Authorization is also required when he is to be arrested.
3. A deputy may be detained or arrested without authorization when he is apprehended during or immediately after the commission of a serious crime. In these cases, the General Prosecutor immediately notifies the Assembly, which, when it determines that the proceeding is unjustified, decides to lift the measure.
4. In the cases contemplated in paragraphs 2 and 3 of this article, the Assembly decides by secret ballot.

CHAPTER III--ORGANIZATION AND OPERATION

Article 74

1. The Assembly conducts its annual work in two sessions. The first session begins on the third Monday of January and the second session on the first Monday of September.
2. The Assembly meets in extraordinary session when requested by the President of the Republic, the Prime Minister or by one- fifth of all the deputies.
3. Extraordinary sessions are called by the Speaker of the Assembly on the basis of a defined agenda.

Article 75

1. The Assembly elects and discharges its Speaker.
2. The Assembly is organized and operates according to regulations approved by a majority of all its members.

Article 76

1. The Speaker chairs debates, directs the work, assures respect for the rights of the Assembly and its members, and represents the Assembly in relations with others.
2. The highest civil employee of the Assembly is the General Secretary.

3. Other services necessary for the operation of the Assembly are carried out by other employees, as specified by internal regulations.

Article 77

1. The Assembly elects standing committees from its ranks and may also establish special committees.
2. The Assembly has the right and, upon the request of one- fourth of its members, is obliged to designate investigatory committees to review a particular issue. Their conclusions are not binding on the courts, but they may be made known to the office of the prosecutor, which evaluates them according to legal procedures.
3. Investigatory committees operate according to procedures set by law.

Article 78

1. The Assembly takes decisions by a majority of votes, in the presence of more than half of its members, except for cases where the Constitution provides for a qualified majority.
2. Meetings of the deputies that are convened without being called in accordance with the regulations do not have any effect.

Article 79

1. Meetings of the Assembly are open.
2. At the request of the President of the Republic, the Prime Minister or one-fifth of the deputies, meetings of the Assembly may be closed when a majority of all its members have voted in favor of it.

Article 80

1. The Prime Minister and any other member of the Council of Ministers must answer interpellances and questions of the deputies within three weeks.
2. A member of the Council of Ministers has the right to take part in meetings of the Assembly or of its committees; he is given the floor whenever he requests it.
3. The heads of state institutions, at the request of the parliamentary committees, give explanations and information about specific issues of their activity to the extent that the law permits.

CHAPTER IV--THE LEGISLATIVE PROCESS

Article 81

1. The Council of Ministers, every deputy and 20,000 electors each have the right to propose laws.
2. There are approved by three- fifths of all members of the Assembly:
    a. the laws for the organization and operation of the institutions contemplated by the Constitution;
    b. the law on citizenship;

c. the law on general and local elections;
ç. the law on referenda;
d. the codes;
dh. the law on the state of emergency;
e. the law on the status of public functionaries; ë. the law on amnesty;
f. the law on administrative divisions of the Republic.

Article 82

1. The proposal of laws, when this is the case, must always be accompanied by a report that justifies the financial costs of its implementation.
2. No non-governmental draft law that makes necessary an increase in the expenses of the state budget or diminishes income may be approved without hearing the opinion of the Council of Ministers, which must be given within 30 days from the date of receiving the draft law.
3. If the Council of Ministers does not give an answer within the above time period, the draft law passes for review according to the normal procedure.

Article 83

1. A draft law is voted on three times: in principle, article by article, and in its entirety.
2. The Assembly may, at the request of the Council of Ministers or one-fifth of all the deputies, review and approve a draft law by an expedited procedure, but no sooner than one week from the beginning of the review procedure.
3. The expedited procedure is not permitted for the review of the draft laws contemplated in Article 81, paragraph 2, with the exception of subparagraph dh.

Article 84

1. The President of the Republic promulgates an approved law within 20 days from its submission.
2. A law is deemed promulgated if the President of the Republic does not exercise the rights provided for in paragraph 1 of this article or in paragraph 1 of article 85.
3. A law enters into force with the passage of not less than 15 days after its publication in the Official Journal.
4. In cases of extraordinary measures, as well as in cases of necessity and emergency, when the Assembly decides with a majority of all its members and the President of the Republic gives his consent, a law enters into force immediately, but only after it is made known publicly. The law shall be published in the first number of the Official Journal.

Article 85

1. The President of the Republic has the right to return a law for re-consideration only once.
2. The decree of the President for the re-consideration of a law loses its effect when a majority of all the members of the Assembly vote against it.

PART FOUR--THE PRESIDENT OF THE R EPUBLIC

Article 86

1. The President of the Republic is the Head of State and represents the unity of the people.
2. Only an Albanian citizen by birth who has resided in Albania for not less than the past 10 years and who has reached the age of 40 may be elected President.

Article 87

1. A candidate for President is proposed to the Assembly by a group of not less than 20 of its members. A member is not permitted to take part in more than one proposing group.
2. The President of the Republic is elected by the Assembly by secret ballot and without debate by a majority of three- fifths of all its members.
3. When this majority is not reached in the first ballot, a second ballot takes place within 7 days from the day of the first ballot.
4. When this majority is not reached even in the second ballot, a third ballot takes place within 7 days.
5. When there is more than one candidate and none of them has received the required majority, within 7 days, a fourth ballot takes place between the two candidates who have received the greatest number of votes.
6. If even in the fourth ballot neither of the two candidates has received the required majority, a fifth ballot takes place.
7. If even in the fifth ballot neither of the two candidates has received the required majority, the Assembly is dissolved and new general elections take place within 60 days.
8. The new Assembly elects the President pursuant to the procedure contemplated in paragraphs 1 to 7 of this article. If even the new Assembly fails to elect the President, the Assembly is dissolved and new general elections take place within 60 days.
9. The subsequent Assembly elects the President of the Republic by a majority of all its members.

Article 88

1. The President of the Republic is in every case elected for 5 years, with the right to be reelected only once.
2. The procedure for the election of the President begins no later than 30 days before the end of the previous presidential mandate.
3. The President begins his duties after he takes the oath before the Assembly, but not before the mandate of the President who is leaving has been completed. The President takes this oath:
"I swear that I will obey the Constitution and laws of the country, I will respect the rights and freedoms of citizens, I will protect the independence of the Republic, and I will serve the general interest and the progress of the Albanian People." The President may add: "So help me God!"
4. A President who resigns before the end of his mandate may not be a candidate in the presidential election that takes place after his resignation.

Article 89

The President of the Republic may not hold any other public position, may not be a member of a party and may not carry out other private activity.

Article 90

1. The President of the Republic is not responsible for actions carried out in the exercise of his duty.
2. The President of the Republic may be dismissed for serious violations of the Constitution and for the commission of a serious crime. In these cases, a proposal for the dismissal of the President may be made by not less than one- fourth of the members of the Assembly and shall be supported by not less than two-thirds of all its members.
3. The decision of the Assembly is sent to the Constitutional Court, which, when it verifies the guilt of the President of the Republic, declares his dismissal from duty.

Article 91

1. When the President of the Republic is temporarily unable to exercise his functions or his place is vacant, the Speaker of the Assembly takes his place and exercises his powers.
2. If the President cannot exercise his duties for more than 60 days, the Assembly decides by two-thirds of all its members to send the issue to the Constitutional Court, which determines conclusively the fact of his incapacity. In the case of a determination of incapacity, the place of the President remains vacant and the election of a new President begins within 10 days from the date of determination of incapacity.

Article 92

The President also exercises these powers:
a. he addresses messages to the Assembly;
b. he exercises the right of pardon according to law;
c. he grants Albanian citizenship and permits it to be relinquished according to law;
ç. he grants decorations and titles of honor according to law;
d. he grants the highest military ranks according to law;
dh. on the proposal of the Prime Minister, he appoints and withdraws plenipotentiary representatives of the Republic of Albania to other states and international organizations;
e. he accepts letters of credential and the withdrawal of diplomatic representatives of other states and international organizations accredited to the Republic of Albania;
ë. he enters into international agreements according to law;
f. on the proposal of the Prime Minister, he appoints the director of the intelligence service of the state;
g. he nominates the Chairman of the Academy of Sciences and the rectors of universities pursuant to law;
gj. he sets the date of the elections for the Assembly, for the organs of local power and for the conduct of referenda;
h. he requests opinions and information in writing from the directors of state institutions for issues that relate to their duties.

Article 93

The President of the Republic issues decrees in the exercise of his powers.

Article 94

The President of the Republic may not exercise other powers besides those contemplated expressly by the Constitution and granted by laws issued in compliance with it.

PART FIVE--THE COUNCIL OF MINISTERS

Article 95

1. The Council of Ministers consists of the Prime Minister, the deputy prime minister, and the ministers.
2. The Council of Ministers exercises every state function that is not given to the organs of other state powers or of local government.

Article 96

1. At the beginning of a legislature, as well as when the position of Prime Minister is vacant, the President of the Republic appoints the Prime Minister on the proposal of the party or coalition of parties that has the majority of seats in the Assembly.
2. If the Prime Minister appointed is not approved by the Assembly, the President appoints a new Prime Minister within 10 days.
3. If the newly appointed Prime Minister is not approved by the Assembly, the Assembly elects another Prime Minister within 10 days. In this case, the President appoints the new Prime Minister.
4. If the Assembly fails to elect a new Prime Minister, the President of the Republic dissolves the Assembly.

Article 97

Within 10 days, the Prime Minister appointed according to article 96, article 104 or article 105 presents the political program of the Council of Ministers, together with its composition, to the Assembly for approval.

Article 98

1. A minister is appointed and dismissed by the President of the Republic, on the proposal of the Prime Minister, within 7 days.
2. The decree is reviewed by the Assembly within 10 days.

Article 99

Before taking office, the Prime Minister, the deputy prime minister, and the ministers take an oath before the President of the Republic.

Article 100

1. The Council of Ministers determines the principal general policies of the state.

2. The Council of Ministers takes decisions upon the proposal of the Prime Minister or the respective minister.
3. Meetings of the Council of Ministers are held behind closed doors.
4. Acts of the Council of Ministers are valid when signed by the Prime Minister and the proposing minister.
5. The Council of Ministers issues decisions and instructions.

Article 101

In cases of necessity and emergency, the Council of Ministers may issue, under its own responsibility, normative acts having the force of law for taking temporary measures. These normative acts are immediately submitted to the Assembly, which is convened within 5 days if it is not in session. These acts lose force retroactively if they are not approved by the Assembly within 45 days.

Article 102

1. The Prime Minister:
    a. represents the Council of Ministers and chairs its meetings;
    b. outlines and presents the principal general policies of the state and is responsible for them;
    c. assures the implementation of legislation and policies approved by the Council of Ministers;
    ç. coordinates and supervises the work of the members of the Council of Ministers and other institutions of the central state administration;
    d. performs other duties contemplated in the Constitution and laws.
2. The Prime Minister resolves disagreements among ministers.
3. The Prime Minister issues orders in the exercise of his powers.
4. Within the principal general policies of the state, a minister directs, under his responsibility, activities within his competency. A minister issues orders and instructions in the exercise of his powers.

Article 103

1. Anyone who is eligible to be a deputy may be appointed a minister.
2. A minister may not exercise any other state activity or be a director or member of the organs of profit- making companies.
3. Members of the Council of Ministers enjoy the immunity of a deputy.

Article 104

1. If a motion of confidence presented by the Prime Minister is rejected by a majority of all members of the Assembly, the Assembly elects another Prime Minister within 15 days. In this case, the President appoints the new Prime Minister.
2. When the Assembly fails to elect a new Prime Minister, the President of the Republic dissolves the Assembly.
3. The vote on the motion cannot take place if three days have not passed from the day it was presented.

Article 105

1. If a motion of no confidence presented by one-fifth of the members of the Assembly is approved by a majority of all its members, the Assembly elects another Prime Minister within 15 days. In this case, the President appoints the new Prime Minister.
2. When the Assembly fails to elect a new Prime Minister, the President of the Republic dissolves the Assembly.
3. The vote on the motion cannot take place if three days have not passed from the day it was presented.

Article 106

The Prime Minister and the ministers are obligated to stay in office until the formation of the succeeding Council of Ministers.

Article 107

1. Public employees apply the law and are at the service of the people.
2. Employees in the public administration are selected by competition, except when the law provides otherwise.
3. Guarantees of tenure and legal treatment of public employees are regulated by law.

PART SIX--LOCAL GOVERNMENT

Article 108

1. Communes or municipalities and regions are the units of local government. Other units of local government are regulated by law.
2. The territorial-administrative division of the units of local government is established by law on the basis of mutual economic needs and interests, and of historical tradition. Their borders may not be changed without first hearing the opinion of their inhabitants.
3. Communes and municipalities are basic units of local government. They perform all the duties of self-government, with the exception of those that are given by law to other units of local government.
4. Self-government in the local units is exercised through their representative organs and local referenda. The principles and procedures for the conduct of local referenda are provided by law in accordance with article 151, paragraph 2.

Article 109

1. The representative organs of the basic units of local government are the councils, which are elected every four years by direct general elections and by secret ballot.

2. The executive organ of a municipality or commune is the mayor, who is elected directly by the people in the manner contemplated in paragraph 1 of this article.
3. Only citizens with permanent residence in the territory of the respective local unit have the right to be elected to the local councils and as mayor of the municipality or commune.
4. The organs of local government units have the right to form unions and joint institutions with one another for the representation of their interests, to cooperate with local units of other countries, and to be represented in international organizations of local governments.

Article 110

1. A region consists of several basic units of local government with traditional, economic and social ties and common interests.
2. The region is the unit where regional policies are made and implemented and where they are harmonized with policies of the state.
3. The representative organ of the region is the regional council. Municipalities and communes delegate members to the regional council in proportion to their population, but in any case at least one member. The mayors of communes and municipalities are always members of the regional council. Other members are elected through proportional lists from among the municipal or communal councilors by the respective councils.
4. The Regional Council has the right to issue ordinances and decisions with general binding force for the region.

Article 111

1. The units of local government are juridical persons.
2. The units of local government have an independent budget, which is set in the manner provided by law.

Article 112

1. Powers of the state administration may be delegated by law to the units of local government. Expenses that are incurred in the exercise of the delegation are covered by the state.
2. Obligations may be imposed on the organs of local government only in compliance with law or according to agreements entered into by them. Expenses related to the obligations imposed by law on the organs of local government are covered by the state budget.

Article 113

1. The communal, municipal and regional councils:
    a. regulate and administer in an independent manner local issues within their jurisdiction;
    b. exercise property rights, administer their income independently, and are entitled to exercise economic activity;
    c. have the right to collect and spend income necessary for the exercise of their functions;
    ç. have the right, in compliance with law, to establish local taxes as well as their level;
    d. establish rules for their organization and operation in compliance with law;
    dh. create symbols of local government and local titles of honor;

e. undertake initiatives for local issues before the organs set by law.
2. The organs of units of local government issue ordinances, decisions and orders.
3. The rights of self- government of the units of local government are protected in court.

Article 114

The Council of Ministers appoints a prefect as its representative in every region. The powers of the prefect are set by law.

Article 115

1. A directly elected organ of a local government unit may be dissolved or discharged by the Council of Ministers for serious violations of the Constitution or the laws.
2. The dissolved or discharged organ may complain, within 15 days, to the Constitutional Court, in which case the decision of the Council of Ministers is suspended.
3. If the right to complain is not exercised within 15 days, or if the Constitutional Court upholds the decision of the Council of Ministers, the President of the Republic sets a date for elections in the respective local unit.

PART SEVEN--NORMATIVE ACTS AND INTERNATIONAL AGREEMENTS

CHAPTER I--NORMATIVE ACTS

Article 116

1. Normative acts that are effective in the entire territory of the Republic of Albania are:
   a. the Constitution;
   b. ratified international agreements;
   c. the laws;
   ç. normative acts of the Council of Ministers.
2. Acts that are issued by the organs of local government are effective only within the territorial jurisdiction of these organs.
3. Normative acts of ministers and directors of other central institutions are effective within the sphere of their jurisdiction in the entire territory of the Republic of Albania.

Article 117

1. The laws and the normative acts of the Council of Ministers, ministers and other central state institutions acquire legal effect only after they are published in the Official Journal.
2. The promulgation and publication of other normative acts is done in the manner provided by law.
3. International agreements that are ratified by law are promulgated and published according to the procedures contemplated for laws. The promulgation and publication of other international agreements is done according to law.

Article 118

1. Substatutory acts are issued on the basis of and for implementation of the laws by the organs provided in the Constitution.
2. A law shall authorize the issuance of substatutory acts, designate the competent organ, the issues that are to be regulated, and the principles on the basis of which the substatutory acts are issued.
3. The organ authorized by law to issue substatutory acts as is specified in paragraph 2 of this article may not delegate its power to another organ.

Article 119

1. The rules of the Council of Ministers, of the ministries and other central institutions, as well as orders of the Prime Minister, the ministers and the heads of central institutio ns, have an internal character and are binding only on their subordinate administrative entities.
2. These acts are issued on the basis of law and may not serve as a basis for taking decisions that affect individuals and other subjects.
3. Rules and orders are issued on the basis of and for the implementation of acts that have general legal effect.

Article 120

The principles and procedures for the issuance of local legal acts are provided by law.

CHAPTER II--INTERNATIONAL AGREEMENTS

Article 121

1. The ratification and denunciation of international agreements by the Republic of Albania is done by law when they involve:
    a. territory, peace, alliances, political and military issues;
    b. human rights and freedoms, and obligations of citizens as provided in the Constitutio n;
    c. the membership of the Republic of Albania in international organizations;
    ç. the assumption of financial obligations by the Republic of Albania;
    d. the approval, amendment or repeal of laws.
2. The Assembly may, by a majority of all its members, ratify other international agreements that are not contemplated in paragraph 1 of this article.
3. The Prime Minister notifies the Assembly whenever the Council of Ministers signs an international agreement that is not ratified by law.
4. The principles and procedures for ratification and denunciation of international agreements are provided by law.

Article 122

1. Any ratified international agreement constitutes part of the internal legal system after it is published in the Official Journal of the Republic of Albania. It is directly applicable, except when it is not self-executing and its application requires the adoption of a law. The amendment and repeal of laws approved by a majority of all members of the

Assembly is done by the same majority for the purposes of the ratification of an international agreement.
2. An international agreement ratified by law has priority over the laws of the country that are incompatible with it.
3. The norms issued by an international organization have priority, in case of conflict, over the law of the country when the direct application of the norms issued by the organization is expressly contemplated in the agreement ratified by the Republic of Albania for participation therein.

Article 123

1. The Republic of Albania delegates to international organizations state powers for specific issues on the basis of international agreements.
2. The law that ratifies an international agreement as provided in paragraph 1 of this article is approved by a majority of all members of the Assembly.
3. The Assembly may decide that the ratification of such an agreement be done through a referendum.

PART EIGHT--CONSTITUTIONAL COURT

Article 124

1. The Constitutional Court guarantees respect for the Constitution and interprets it conclusively.
2. The Constitutional Court is subject only to the Constitution.

Article 125

1. The Constitutional Court is composed of nine members, who are appointed by the President of the Republic with the consent of the Assembly.
2. Judges are named for nine years without the right to be reelected, among lawyers with high qualifications and with professional work experience of not less than fifteen years.
3. One-third of the composition of the Constitutional Court is renewed every three years, according to the procedure determined by law.
4. The President of the Constitutional Court is appointed for a 3-year term from the ranks of its members by the President of the Republic with the consent of the Assembly.
5. A judge of the Constitutional Court continues in office until the appointment of his successor.

Article 126

A judge of the Constitutional Court cannot be criminally prosecuted without the consent of the Constitutional Court. A judge of the Constitutional Court can be detained or arrested only if apprehended while committing a crime or immediately after its commission. The competent organ notifies the Constitutional Court immediately. If the Constitutional Court does not give its consent within 24 hours to bring the arrested judge to court, the competent organ is obliged to release him.

Article 127

1. The mandate of a judge of the Constitutional Court ends when:
   a. he is sentenced by a final court decision for commission of a crime;
   b. he fails to appear for duty, without reason, for more than 6 months;
   c. he reaches 70 years of age;
   ç. he resigns;
   d. he is declared incapable of acting by a final court decision.
2. The end of the mandate of a judge is declared by a decision of the Constitutional Court.
3. In the case of a vacancy, the President of the Republic with the consent of the Assembly appoints a new judge, who remains in office until the end of the mandate of the departed judge.

Article 128

A judge of the Constitutional Court can be removed by the Assembly by two-thirds of all its members for violation of the Constitution, commission of a crime, mental or physical incapacity, or acts and behavior that seriously discredit judicial integrity and reputation. The decision of the Assembly is reviewed by the Constitutional Court, which, when it determines the existence of one of these grounds, declares the removal from office of the member of the Constitutional Court.

Article 129

A judge of the Constitutional Court takes office after taking an oath before the President of the Republic.

Article 130

Being a judge of the Constitutional Court is incompatible with any other state, political or private activity.

Article 131

The Constitutional Court decides on:
a. the compatibility of a law with the Constitution or with international agreements as provided in article 122;
b. the compatibility of international agreements with the Cons titution, prior to their ratification;
c. the compatibility of normative acts of the central and local organs with the Constitution and international agreements;
ç. conflicts of competencies among the powers as well as between central government and local government;
d. the constitutionality of parties and other political organizations, as well as their activity, according to article 9 of this Constitution;
dh. removal from office of the President of the Republic and verification of his inability to exercise his functions;
e. issues related to the eligibility and incompatibilities in exercising the functions of the President of the Republic and of the deputies, as well as the verification of their election;

ë. the constitutionality of a referendum and the verification of its results;
f. the final adjudication of the complaints of individuals for the violation of their constitutional rights to due process of law, after all legal remedies for the protection of those rights have been exhausted.

Article 132

1. The decisions of the Constitutional Court have general binding force and are final. The Constitutional Court can only invalidate the acts it reviews.
2. The decisions of the Constitutional Court enter into force on the day of their publication in the Official Journal, unless the Constitutional Court has decided that the law or normative act be invalidated on another date. A dissenting opinion is published together with the decision.

Article 133

1. The acceptance of complaints for adjudication is decided by the number of judges determined by law.
2. The Constitutional Court takes decisions by a majority of all its members.

Article 134

1. The Constitutional Court initiates a proceeding only on the request of:
   a. the President of the Republic;
   b. the Prime Minister;
   c. not less than one- fifth of the deputies;
   ç. the head of High State Control;
   d. any court, under article 145, paragraph 2 of this Constitution;
   dh. the People's Advocate;
   e. the organs of local government;
   ë. the organs of religious communities;
   f. political parties and other organizations;
   g. individuals.
2. The subjects contemplated in subparagraphs dh, e, ë, f and g of paragraph 1 of this article may make a request only for issues related to their interests.

PART NINE--THE COURTS

Article 135

1. The judicial power is exercised by the High Court, as well as by the courts of appeal and courts of first instance, which are established by law.
2. The Assembly may by law establish courts for particular areas, but in no case an extraordinary court.

Article 136

1. The members of the High Court are appointed by the President of the Republic with the consent of the Assembly.
2. One of the members is appointed President following the procedure contemplated by paragraph 1 of this article.
3. The President and members of the High Court hold office for 9 years without the right of re-appointment.
4. The other judges are appointed by the President of the Republic upon the proposal of the High Council of Justice.
5. Only citizens with higher legal education may be judges. The conditions and procedures for selection are defined by law.

Article 137

1. A judge of the High Court may be criminally prosecuted only with the approval of the Assembly.
2. A judge of the High Court may be detained or arrested only if apprehended while committing a crime or immediately after its commission. The competent organ notifies the Constitutional Court immediately. If the Constitutional Court does not consent within 24 hours to bring the arrested judge before a court, the competent organ is obliged to release him.
3. Other judges may be criminally prosecuted only with the approval of the High Council of Justice.
4. A judge may be detained or arrested only if apprehended while committing a crime or immediately after its commission. The competent organ notifies the High Council of Justice immediately. If the High Council of Justice does not consent within 24 hours to bringing the arrested judge before a court, the competent organ is obliged to release him.

Article 138

The time judges stay in office cannot be limited; their pay and other benefits cannot be lowered.

Article 139

1. The mandate of a High Court judge ends when:
   a. he is convicted of a crime by a final court decision;
   b. fails to appear for duty, without reason, for more than six months;
   c. he reaches 65 years of age;
   ç. he resigns;
   d. he is declared incapable of acting by a final court decision.
2. The end of the mandate of a judge is declared by a decision of the High Court.

Article 140

A judge of the High Court may be removed by the Assembly by two-thirds of all its members for violation of the Constitution, commission of a crime, mental or physical incapacity, or acts and behavior that seriously discredit judicial integrity and reputation. The decision of the Assembly is reviewed by the Constitutional Court, which, when it determines the existence of one of these grounds, declares his removal from office.

Article 141

1. The High Court has original and review jurisdiction. It has original jurisdiction when adjudicating criminal charges against the President of the Republic, the Prime Minister, members of the Council of Ministers, deputies, judges of the High Court, and judges of the Constitutional Court.
2. For the unification or amendment of judicial practice, the High Court has the right to select particular judicial cases for review in the joint colleges.

Article 142

1. Judicial decisions shall be reasoned.
2. The High Court shall publish its decisions as well as the minority opinions.
3. State organs must execute judicial decisions.

Article 143

Being a judge is incompatible with any other state, political or private activity.

Article 144

Courts have a separate budget, which they administer themselves. They propose their budget according to law.

Article 145

1. Judges are independent and subject only to the Constitution and the laws.
2. If judges believe that a law is unconstitutional, they do not apply it. In this case, they suspend the proceedings and send the question to the Constitutional Court. Decisions of the Constitutional Court are binding on all courts.
3. Interference in the activity of the courts or of the judges entails liability according to law.

Article 146

1. Courts render decisions in the name of the Republic.
2. In every case judicial decisions are announced publicly.

Article 147

1. The High Council of Justice consists of the President of the Republic, the President of the High Court, the Minister of Justice, three members elected by the Assembly, and nine judges of all levels elected by the National Judicial Conference. Elected members stay in office for five years, without the right of immediate reelection.
2. The President of the Republic is the Chairman of the High Council of Justice.
3. The High Council of Justice, on the proposal of the President, elects a vice-chairman from its ranks. The vice-chairman organizes the activity of the High Council of Justice and chairs its meetings in the absence of the President of the Republic.

4. The High Council of Justice decides on the transfer of judges as well as their disciplinary responsibility pursuant to law.
5. Transfer of judges may not be done without their consent, except when the need for reorganization of the judicial system requires it.
6. A judge may be removed by the High Council of Justice for commission of a crime, mental or physical incapacity, acts and behavior that seriously discredit judicial integrity and reputation, or professional insufficiency. The judge has the right to appeal this decision to the High Court, which decides in the joint colleges.

PART TEN--THE OFFICE OF THE PROSECUTOR

Article 148

1. The office of the prosecutor exercises criminal prosecution and represents the accusation in court on behalf of the state. The office of the prosecutor also performs other duties set by law.
2. Prosecutors are organized and operate as a centralized organ attached to the judicial system.
3. In the exercise of their powers, prosecutors are subject to the Constitution and the laws.

Article 149

1. The General Prosecutor is appointed by the President of the Republic with the consent of the Assembly.
2. The General Prosecutor may be discharged by the President of the Republic on the proposal of the Assembly for violations of the Constitution or serious violations of the law during the exercise of his duties, for mental or physical incapacity, and for acts and behavior that seriously discredit prosecutorial integrity and reputation.
3. The other prosecutors are appointed and dismissed by the President of the Republic on the proposal of the General Prosecutor.
4. The General Prosecutor informs the Assembly periodically on the condition of criminality.

PART ELEVEN--R EFERENDUM

Article 150

1. The people, through 50,000 citizens entitled to vote, have the right to a referendum for the abrogation of a law, and to request the President of the Republic to call a referendum on issues of special importance.
2. The Assembly, on the proposal of not less than one- fifth of the deputies or on the proposal of the Council of Ministers, can decide that an issue or a draft law of special importance be submitted to referendum.
3. Principles and procedures for conducting a referendum, and its validity, are provided by law.

Article 151

1. A law approved by referendum is promulgated by the President of the Republic.
2. Issues related to the territorial integrity of the Republic of Albania, the limitation of fundamental human rights and freedoms, the budget, taxes and financial obligations of the state, the imposition or lifting of a state of emergency, a declaration of war or peace, and amnesty cannot be submitted to a referendum.
3. A referendum on the same issue cannot be repeated before three years have passed.

Article 152

1. Within 60 days, the Constitutional Court reviews preliminarily the constitutionality of the issues submitted to referendum according to article 150, paragraphs 1 and 2, article 151, paragraphs 2 and 3, and article 177, paragraphs 4 and 5.
2. The importance of the special issues contemplated in paragraphs 1 and 2 of article 150 is not subject to adjudication by the Constitutional Court.
3. The President of the Republic sets the date of the referendum within 45 days after the announcement of a positive decision of the Constitutional Court or after the expiration of the period within which the Constitutional Court should have rendered its decision. During the year, referenda can be held on only one day.

PART TWELVE--CENTRAL ELECTION COMMISSION

Article 153

The Central Election Commission is a permanent organ that prepares, supervises, manages, and verifies all aspects of elections and referenda and announces their results.

Article 154

1. The Commission consists of 9 members elected for a 7-year term. 4 members are elected by the Assembly, two by the President of the Republic, and the 3 other members by the High Council of Justice.
2. The composition of the Central Election Commission is renewed pursuant to the procedure established by law.
3. Membership in the Commission is incompatible with any other state or political activity.
4. Electoral subjects appoint representatives to the Commission. They do not have the right to vote.
5. A member of the Commission enjoys the same immunity as a member of the High Court.
6. The Commission has its own budget.

PART THIRTEEN--PUBLIC FINANCES

Article 155

Fees, taxes and financial obligations, national or local, a reduction of or exemption from them for certain categories of taxpayers and the method of collecting them are set by law. In such cases, the law may not have retroactive effect.

Article 156

The state can make and guarantee loans and financial credits when authorized by law.

Article 157

1. The budgetary system consists of the state budge t and local budgets.
2. The state budget is created by revenues collected from taxes, fees and other financial obligations, and from other lawful revenues. It includes all the expenses of the state.
3. Local organs impose and collect taxes and other obligations as provided by law.
4. The organs of central and local government must make their revenues and expenses public.

Article 158

1. The Prime Minister, on behalf of the Council of Ministers, presents the draft law on the budget to the Assembly during the autumn session, which cannot close without approving it.
2. If the draft law is not approved by the beginning of the next fiscal year, the Council of Ministers applies one-twelfth of the budget of the previous year every month until the new budget is approved.
3. The Assembly approves the new budget within three months from the last day of the previous fiscal year, except when extraordinary measures have been imposed.
4. The Council of Ministers must submit a report to the Assembly on the implementation of the budget and the state debt of the previous year.
5. The Assembly takes a final decision after hearing the report of the High State Control.

Article 159

Principles and procedures for preparing the draft budget and for implementing the budget are defined by law.

Article 160

1. The Assembly may amend the budget during the fiscal year.
2. Amendments to the budget are made according to the procedures provided for drafting and approving it.

3. Expenditures contemplated in other laws cannot be reduced so long as these laws are in force.

Article 161

1. The Central Bank of the state is the Bank of Albania. It has the exclusive right to issue and circulate Albanian money, to implement monetary policy independently, and to maintain and administer the foreign currency reserves of the Republic of Albania.
2. The Bank of Albania is managed by a council, which is chaired by the Governor. The Governor is elected by the Assembly, on the proposal of the President of the Republic, for seven years with the right of reelection.

PART FOURTEEN--THE HIGH STATE CONTROL

Article 162

1. The High State Control is the highest institution of economic and financial audit. It is subject only to the Constitution and laws.
2. The Chairman of the High State Control is elected and dismissed by the Assembly on the proposal of the President of the Republic. He remains in office for seven years, with the right of reelection.

Article 163

The High State Control audits and reviews:
   a. the economic activity of state institutions and other juridical persons of the state;
   b. the use and protection of state funds by organs of central and local government;
   c. the economic activity of juridical persons in which the state owns more than half of the interest, or whose debts, credits, and obligations are guaranteed by the state.

Article 164

1. The High State Control submits to the Assembly:
   a. a report on the implementation of the state budget;
   b. its opinion on the report of the Council of Ministers for the expenses of the previous financial year, before it is approved by the Assembly;
   c. information on the results of audits and reviews whenever asked by the Assembly.
2. The High State Control submits an annual report on its activities to the Assembly.

Article 165

1. The Chairman of the High State Control may be invited to participate and speak in the meetings of the Council of Ministers when questions related to its functions are reviewed.
2. The Chairman of the High State Control has the immunity of a member of the High Court.

PART FIFTEEN--ARMED FORCES

Article 166

1. Albanian citizens have the duty to participate in the defense of the Republic of Albania, as provided by law.
2. A citizen who, for reasons of conscience, refuses to serve with weapons in the armed forces is obliged to perform alternative service, as provided by law.

Article 167

1. Military servicemen on active duty cannot be elected or appointed to other state duties or take part in political activity or in a party.
2. Members of the armed forces or persons who perform alternative service enjoy all the constitutional rights and freedoms, except when the law provides otherwise.

Article 168

1. The Armed Forces of the Republic of Albania are composed of the army, navy, and air force.
2. The President of the Republic is the Commander-in-Chief of the Armed Forces.
3. The National Security Council is an advisory orga n of the President of the Republic.

Article 169

1. In time of peace the President of the Republic exercises command of the Armed Forces through the Prime Minister and the Minister of Defense.
2. In time of war the President of the Republic appoints and dismisses the Commander of the Armed Forces on the proposal of the Prime Minister.
3. On the proposal of the Prime Minister, the President of the Republic appoints and dismisses the Chief of the General Staff, and on the proposal of the Minister of Defense he appoints and dismisses the commanders of the army, navy, and air force.
4. The powers of the President of the Republic as Commander- in-Chief of the Armed Forces and those of the Commander of the Armed Forces, and their subordination to the constitutional organs, are defined by law.

PART SIXTEEN--EXTRAORDINARY M EASURES

Article 170

1. Extraordinary measures can be imposed because of a state of war, a state of emergency, or a state of natural disaster and last for as long as these conditions continue.
2. The principles of operation of public organs, and the extent of the restriction of human rights and freedoms during the existence of the situations that require extraordinary measures, are defined by law.
3. A law shall define the principles, areas, and manner of compensation for losses caused as a result of the restriction of human rights and freedoms during the period in which extraordinary measures are imposed.

4. Actions taken as a result of extraordinary measures shall be in proportion to the level of risk and shall aim at re-establishing conditions for the normal operation of the state as soon as possible.
5. During situations that require the imposition of extraordinary measures, none of the following acts may be changed: the Constitution, the laws on the election of the Assembly and of local government organs, and the laws on extraordinary measures.
6. During the period of extraordinary measures, local elections may not be held, a referendum may not be held, and a new President of the Republic may not be elected. Local elections may be held only where the extraordinary measures are not in effect.

Article 171

1. In the case of armed aggression against the Republic of Albania, the President of the Republic, at the request of the Council of Ministers, declares a state of war.
2. In a case of external threat, or when a common defense obligation derives from an international agreement, the Assembly, on the proposal of the President of the Republic, declares a state of war, and imposes a state of general or partial mobilization or demobilization.

Article 172

1. In the case of paragraph 1 of article 171, the President of the Republic submits to the Assembly a decree for establishing a state of war within 48 hours of its signing, specifying the rights that are restricted.
2. The Assembly immediately discusses and decides, by a majority of all its members, upon the decree of the President.

Article 173

1. In the case of a threat to the constitutional order and public security, the Assembly, at the request of the Council of Ministers, may impose a state of emergency in a part or in the whole territory of the State, which lasts for as long as this threat continues, but no longer than 60 days.
2. When a state of emergency is imposed, and if the police are not able to restore order, the Assembly decides to call on the armed forces to intervene.
3. The duration of the state of emergency may be extended only with the consent of the Assembly every 30 days for a period of time not longer than 90 days.

Article 174

1. For preventing or eliminating the consequences of natural disasters or technological accidents, the Council of Ministers may impose for a period of no longer than 30 days a state of natural disaster in a part or the whole territory of the State.
2. A state of natural disaster may be extended only with the consent of the Assembly.

Article 175

1. During a state of war or a state of emergency, the rights and freedoms contemplated by articles 15; 18; 19; 20; 21; 24; 25; 29; 30; 31; 32; 34; 39, paragraph 1; 41, paragraphs 1, 2, 3, and 5; 42; 43; 48; 54; 55 may not be restricted.
2. During a state of natural disaster, the rights and freedoms contemplated by articles 37; 38; 41, paragraph 4; 49; 51 may be restricted.
3. Acts declaring a state of war, emergency or natural disaster shall specify the rights and freedoms that are restricted according to paragraphs 1 and 2 of this article.

Article 176

When the Assembly cannot convene during a state of war, the President of the Republic, on the proposal of the Council of Ministers, may issue acts having the force of law, which shall be approved by the Assembly at its first meeting.

PART SEVENTEEN--AMENDING THE CONSTITUTION

Article 177

1. An initiative for amending the Constitution may be taken by not less than one-fifth of the members of the Assembly.
2. No amendment to the Constitution may take place when extraordinary measures are in effect.
3. A proposed amendment is approved by not less than two-thirds of all members of the Assembly.
4. The Assembly may decide, by two-thirds of all its members, that the proposed constitutional amendments be voted on in a referendum. The proposed constitutional amendment becomes effective after ratification by referendum, which takes place not later than 60 days after its approval by the Assembly.
5. An approved constitutional amendment is submitted to referendum when one-fifth of the members of the Assembly request it.
6. The President of the Republic cannot return for re-consideration a constitutional amendment approved by the Assembly.
7. An amendment approved by referendum is promulgated by the President of the Republic and becomes effective on the date provided for in it.
8. An amendment of the Constitution cannot be made unless a year has passed since the rejection by the Assembly of a proposed amendment on the same issue or three years have passed from its rejection by referendum.

PART EIGHTEEN--TRANSITIONAL AND FINAL PROVISIONS

Article 178

1. Laws and other normative acts approved before the effective date of this Constitution shall be applied as long as they have not been repealed.
2. Draft laws necessary for implementing this Constitution are submitted by the Council of Ministers to the Assembly.

Article 179

1. The mandate of constitutional organs existing on the effective date of this Constitution ends pursuant to the terms contemplated by Law No. 7491, dated 29.04.1991, "On the Major Constitutional Provisions," as amended.
2. The members of the Court of Cassation continue their activity as members of the High Court pursuant to their previous mandate.
3. The members of the High Council of Justice elected from the ranks of the prosecutors are replaced with new members elected by a general meeting of the judges.
4. The organs of local government continue their activity until the end of their mandate.

Article 180

1. International agreements ratified by the Republic of Albania before the effective date of this Constitution are deemed ratified according to this Constitution.
2. The Council of Ministers submits to the Constitutional Court international agreements that contain provisions in conflict with this Constitution.

Article 181

1. Within two to three years from the effective date of this Constitution, the Assembly enacts laws for the just regulation of the various matters related to expropriations and confiscations that took place before the approval of this Constitution, guided by the criteria of article 41.
2. Laws and other normative acts approved before the effective date of this Constitution that relate to expropriations and confiscations shall be applied when they do not conflict with it.

Article 182

Law No. 7491, dated 29.04.1991, "On the Major Constitutional Provisions" and other constitutional laws are repealed on the effective date of this Constitution.

Article 183

This Constitution becomes effective with its promulgation by the President of the Republic.

www.ingramcontent.com/pod-product-compliance
Lightning Source LLC
Chambersburg PA
CBHW031502210526
45463CB00003B/1037